Tim Turtel

The life of a small sea turtle

You love the ocean?

You'll love this story.

Imprint

1. Edition 2023

ISBN 978-3-911121-01-9
Selfpublisher
Author - Doris Kluin

Doris Kluin
c/o IP-Management #20389
Ludwig-Erhard-Str. 18
20459 Hamburg
No Parcels please, return to sender.

© Doris Kluin · All Rights reserved.

Proofreading - ProofreadingServices.com
Mediadesign, retouching & AI prompting - Doris Kluin
e-Mail - Doris.KluinDE@gmail.com

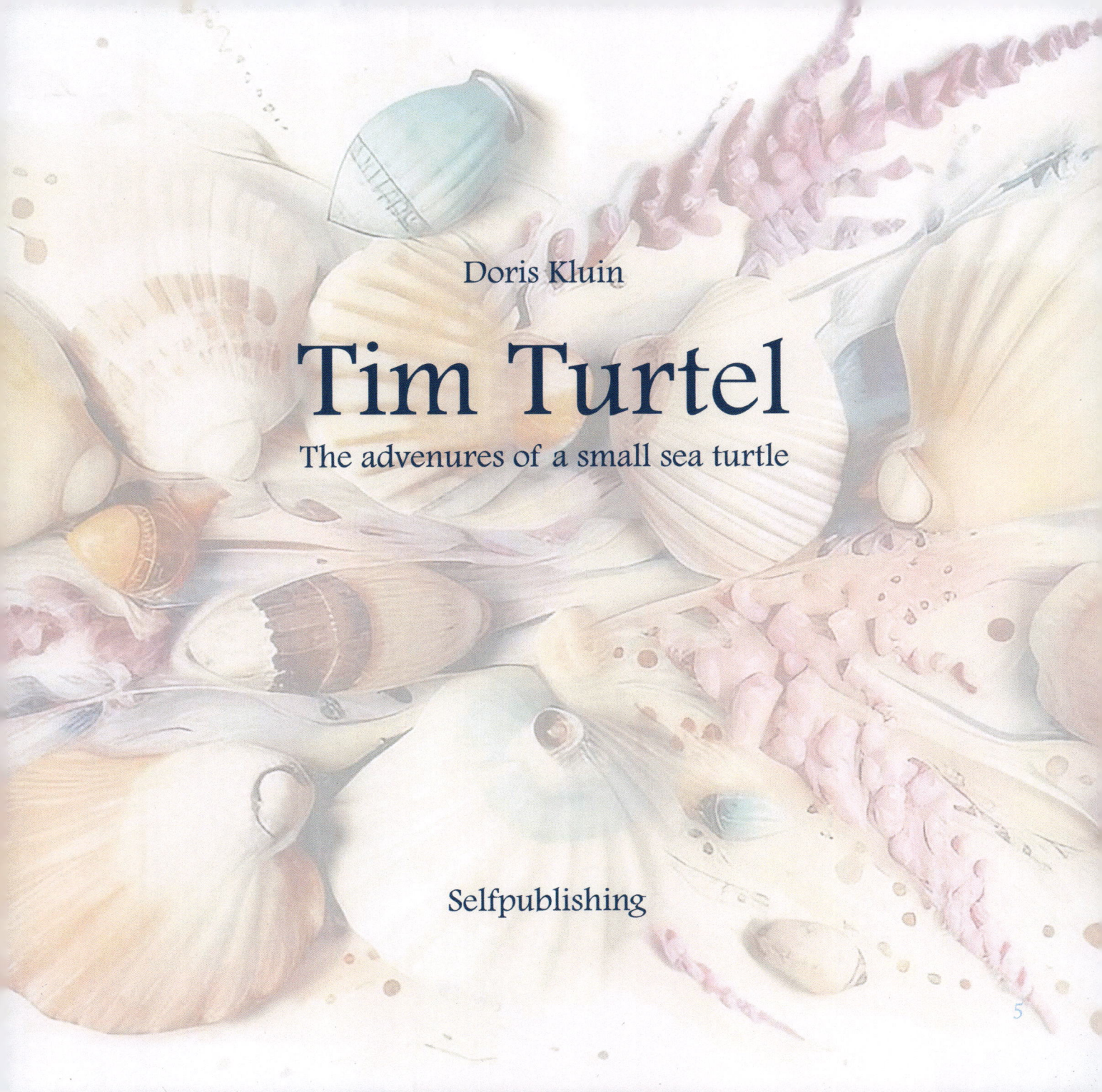

Doris Kluin

Tim Turtel

The advenures of a small sea turtle

Selfpublishing

I'm glad you're here to listen to my story.

You might like it very much. Where do I start?

Ah, yes. Let's start with his name.

Tim, Tim Turtel.

Tim is a sea turtle from the reptile family.
Sea turtles are like normal turtles who live on land,
but in this case, their legs are the fins, and they live
in the sea. In fact, Tim's life also begins on land,
on a beautiful beach in the Caribbean.

Tim's mum comes to the beach one summer night
and lays her eggs in a hollow in the soft sand that
she dug herself. She covers the eggs with sand again.
Then she goes back into the ocean.
The sun incubates the eggs on the beach.

What they will become, boy or girl,
is determined by the temperature.
When it's warm, they will become girls.
When it's a bit colder, they will become boys.

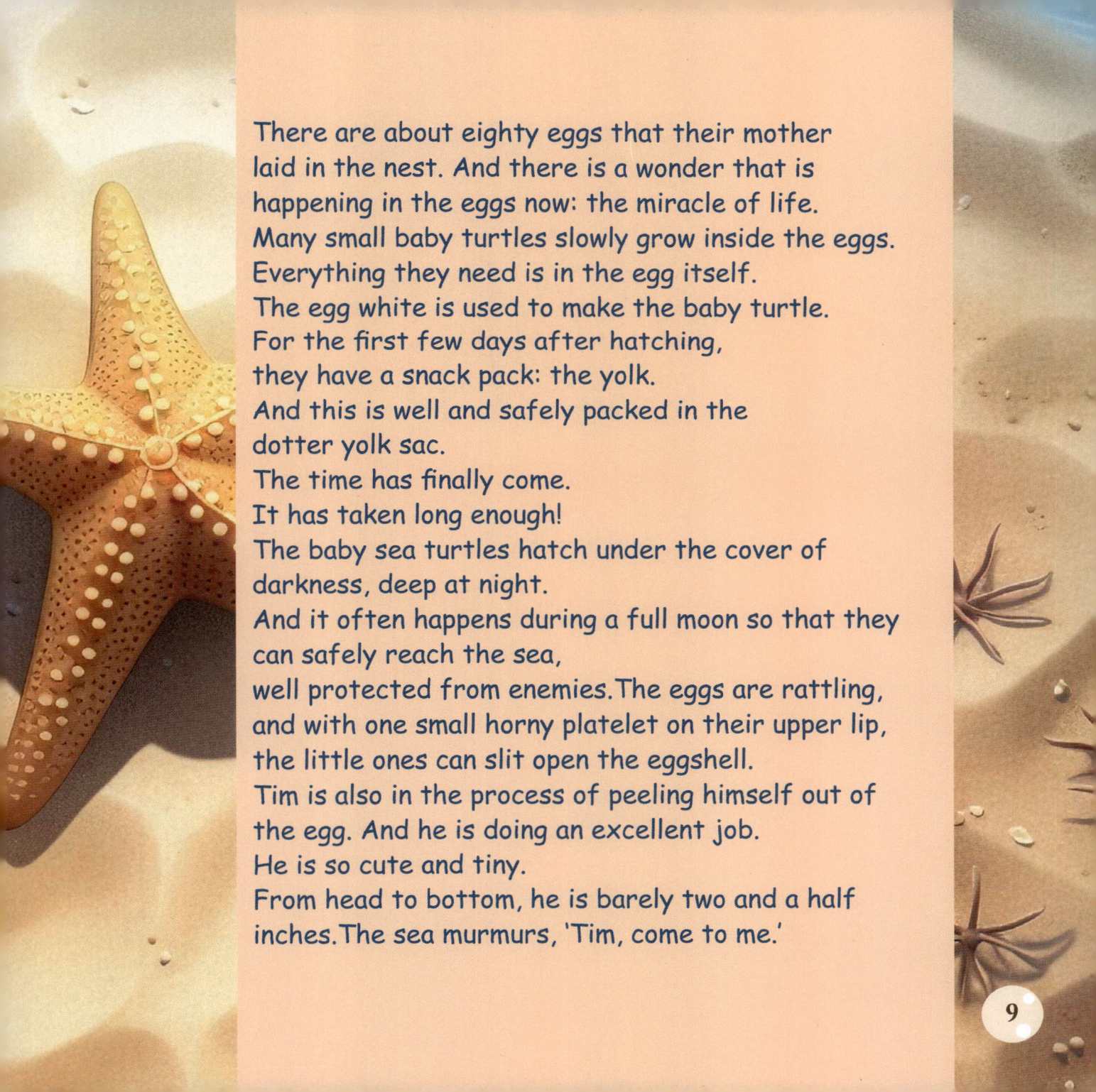

There are about eighty eggs that their mother laid in the nest. And there is a wonder that is happening in the eggs now: the miracle of life. Many small baby turtles slowly grow inside the eggs. Everything they need is in the egg itself.
The egg white is used to make the baby turtle.
For the first few days after hatching,
they have a snack pack: the yolk.
And this is well and safely packed in the dotter yolk sac.
The time has finally come.
It has taken long enough!
The baby sea turtles hatch under the cover of darkness, deep at night.
And it often happens during a full moon so that they can safely reach the sea,
well protected from enemies. The eggs are rattling, and with one small horny platelet on their upper lip, the little ones can slit open the eggshell.
Tim is also in the process of peeling himself out of the egg. And he is doing an excellent job.
He is so cute and tiny.
From head to bottom, he is barely two and a half inches. The sea murmurs, 'Tim, come to me.'

Tim is covered by the darkness of the night like a woollen blanket. He has already become tired from the hard work. Now he needs a little break before he can move on.
But a strange feeling pulls him towards the water.
He hears the sound of the sea and knows immediately where he has to run to.
It's so exciting!
Running is not the right expression because he has fins. And the fins make it difficult for him to move forward in the soft sand. Tim slowly fights his way towards the sea. That is very exhausting!
Tim bravely pushes himself little by little to the sea. The sand beneath him suddenly becomes damp and solid.
In this way, he can make better and, above all, faster progress.
He doesn't know why, but he is rushing before it gets light and before the sun rises.
A wave catches him and pushes him back.
Tim thinks that he will have to crawl that much again. But no. The wave pulls him back into deeper water.
How happy our little Tim Turtel is now!
Swimming is so much easier than crawling.

The night passes quickly. And the sun rises rapidly in the sky. Everything becomes bright, and Tim looks back at the beach. There, he can see a huge red crab.
She calls out to him, 'Hey, you, come back to me!'
And she waves her arms wildly, and her big crab claws clatter very loudly.
But Tim does not react to her.
He just looks and tries to understand what that red thing at the beach is.

'Come back, little sea turtle!' she calls.
And she rattles her sharp claws even louder.
'Who are you?' asks Tim.
'I'm Corallina the crab. I'm hungry. Come on over to me. We can play and eat together.'
But Tim is not stupid.
He has instincts that warn him of danger.
A gut feeling.
Maybe you know this too?

'No, thanks. Your big red scissors hands are looking dangerous. And I'm not hungry,' he replies and dives quickly, far away from the big red crab with the sharp scissors hands.

Learning to dive is the first task for Tim.
He also needs to find out how long the air lasts.
He refuels for air on the surface of the sea.
This goes very nicely and easily. Tim can stay underwater for a very long time, much longer than you can do, I swear. He continues to dive in good spirits.
Then he watches a bunch of big adult turtles.
They look like him.
They are much, much bigger than him.
'Hello, little one!' one of the adult sea turtles calls out to him. 'Be careful and dive a little deeper. Here, there are many big animals that would like to take you for breakfast.'
'Thanks for the tip! I'm Tim. Where are you guys headed?'
'Hello, Tim. We are on a long journey through the ocean. We are going to the green seagrass meadows, where we will stay for the next few months.'
'Can I come with you?' Tim asks them.
'No, you are still too small and too slow. It's better for you to stay here and wait until you've grown up. Take care of yourself, little Tim!'
He looks sad after they disappear in the blue of the sea. He would have loved to come with them.

The adult sea turtles' advice was certainly correct,
Tim thinks. He fetches a large portion of air
on the surface of the sea and starts diving.
The deeper he gets, the darker the water becomes.
And he feels something around him, gently squeezing him.
That is the water pressure and quite normal.

Suddenly, he sees a big soft thing with many arms
in front of him.
One, two, three. . . that's as far as Tim can count.
He can't keep counting.
'Who are you?' asks the stranger.
'My name is Tim, Tim Turtel,' he replies.
'Hello, Tim. What a brave sea turtle you are!
Come closer. I can't hear that well. My name is Oliver.
I'm an octopus. See my tentacles?'
Tim looks at Oliver with all these long arms.
They look soft but also strong.
Slowly, they meander in his direction.
His instincts are kicking in again.
Get out of here! This is dangerous!
'No, I have an important appointment. Goodbye, Oliver!'
Tim calls back. And he dives as fast as he can into
the depths of the ocean.

After some time, Tim reaches a coral reef and observes from a safe distance the surrounding space. Oliver didn't follow him, and little Tim is safe. What a time to be alive! His little heart is still beating wildly, and he presses himself quickly between the corals to hide himself a little more. Nobody knows what is happening next.
The strange thing in front of him says nothing.
It only drifts in the water. It pulsates, gets bigger, and smaller again. And it also progresses only slowly. It must have a lot of time. Tim dares.
'Hello?' Tim whispers. 'I'm Tim. Who are you?'
No answer. It pulsates and bubbles silently.
Good, thinks Tim. *It has no eyes and no mouth.*
And since he can see through his head a little, he sees it has no brain either. It's just there. Tim calms down.
And then he sees more of those gooey things.
They do nothing to him.
They just float silently past him.
And they look pretty at the same time. And peaceful.
Many years later, Tim is told that these things are jellyfish. Most jellyfish are harmless.
Only a few species are poisonous if you touch their tentacles. Tim was wise to keep his distance.

Tim dives even deeper into the ocean.
It gets even darker.
There will be many creatures here too.
Something lights up briefly in purple and yellow
and with quite colourful patches, like in a rainbow.
And it has a deep voice.
'Am I a male? Am I a female? What am I? Am I both?
I'm colourful. Hahaha!'
'Woo-hoo! Well, I'm Tim. And I'm a boy,' Tim calls out.
'Haaa, hahaha! Wait. I'm a male. I'm a female. Look.
Those are eggs there in my belly pouch.'
The seahorse shows its egg bag, and Tim takes
a look inside.
Sure enough, there are tiny eggs inside.
'Are you all right? You seem pretty upset.
What's your name?' asks Tim.
'I don't have a name. I have pronouns,' it says proudly.
'What's that?' asks Tim in amazement.
'What I am. Male. Female. My pronouns are Ma/Fe.
I make the babies. I carry them out. I have to go.
Goodbye, little Tim!'
Tim finds that not knowing about gender or who and
what you must be exhausting. And to have so many
tasks, being father and mother at the same time.

Quickly, Tim is learning which other fish – crab-like, invertebrates, and whatever else swims there –
are dangerous to him and which animals are not.
That's why Tim mostly swims around between the coral reefs and watches the many colourful fishes.
They are so pretty!
Or he is hiding in the tall seagrass meadows
on the ground, which, by the way, are delicious
and what he feeds on. And they are so nourishing
that Tim easily grows bigger and bigger.
His shell is also getting thicker, and smaller predators can no longer try to hunt after him.
And of course, he can also pull his head into his turtle shell, like all turtles do if they are in danger.
Fortunately, no one has tried to eat Tim.
He is always diving faster than his hungry roommates
in the vast ocean.
Time flies by.
Tim is growing and growing.
He has become much stronger than before,
and he can swim and dive much faster now.
He is now a full eight inches tall.
Tim has learned how to use the ocean currents.
They are like the railway, only invisible.

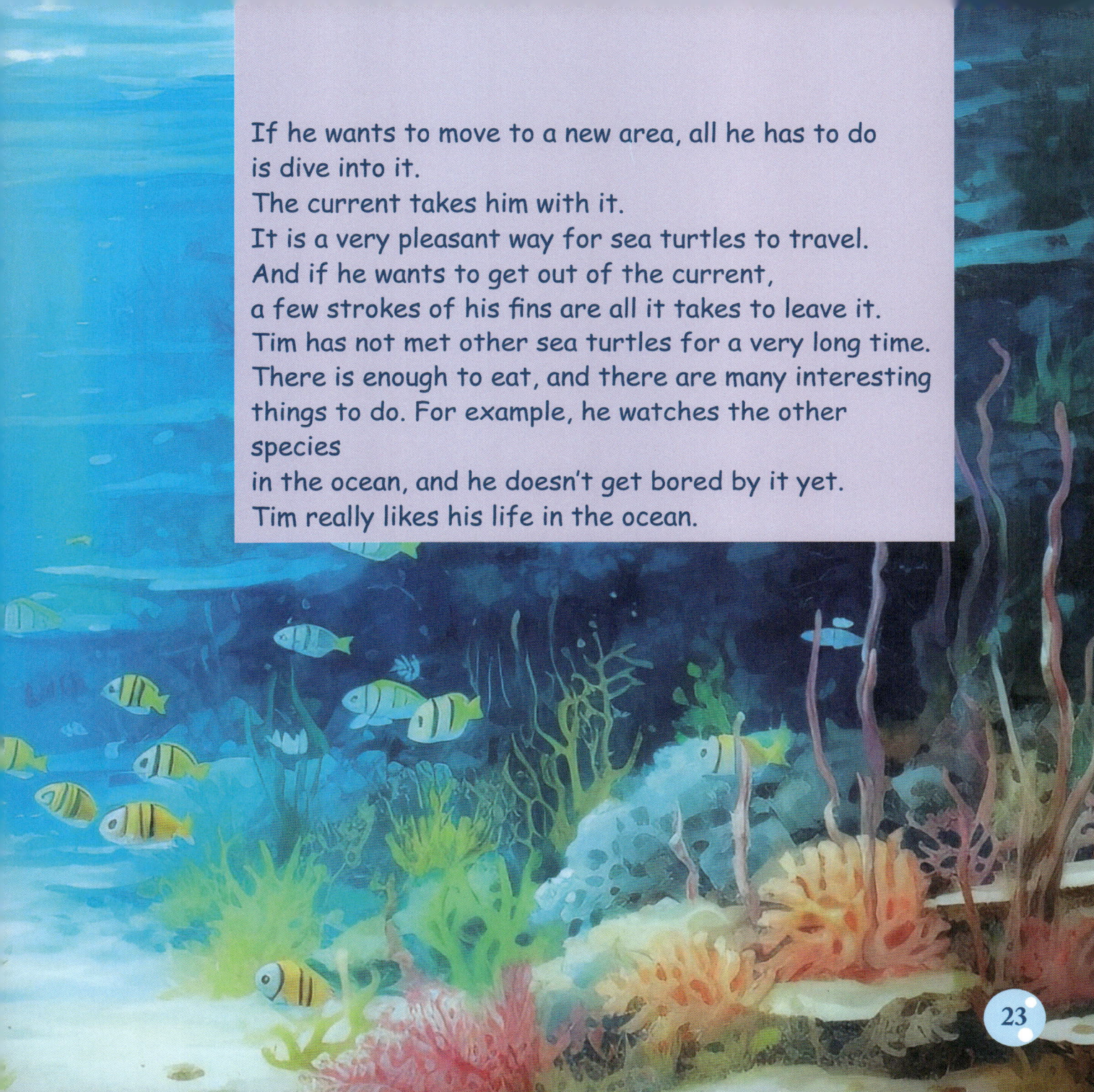

If he wants to move to a new area, all he has to do is dive into it.
The current takes him with it.
It is a very pleasant way for sea turtles to travel.
And if he wants to get out of the current,
a few strokes of his fins are all it takes to leave it.
Tim has not met other sea turtles for a very long time.
There is enough to eat, and there are many interesting things to do. For example, he watches the other species
in the ocean, and he doesn't get bored by it yet.
Tim really likes his life in the ocean.

Tim likes to sleep on the sea surface. Above him is the starry sky. The waves gently rock him, and they push him one way or the other.
But something is different this morning.
It has become cold. Tim sleepily opens his eyes and looks around. Then he wants to dive. He is startled. It doesn't work!
He can't move properly. Only very, very slowly. Reptiles need it to be warm. If it is too cold, their muscles become very stiff. That happens at fifty degrees Fahrenheit and above.
Tim looks around lazily.
No one is there. Then he looks under the water. He hears someone laughing very loudly.
Flihihipeeheeeppper!
'Help! I could use some help here!' Tim shouts.
'Who are you?' the dolphin asks him.
'Tim, Tim Turtel, and I'm stuck here. I can't move!' he answers.
'Cold rigidity. So,' says the second dolphin who has joined in. 'Fortunately, that can't happen to us. We are mammals. We keep ourselves warm by being.'
They swim around him, and Tim gets a little scared.
'Will you please help me now?' he pleads to them.

The dolphins retreat briefly and confer.
After a while, they come back. Phew.
'Yes, we'll help you, little Tim. Watch out.
It can be a bit restless. Better keep your head down.'
Tim closes his eyes tightly.
He is more than a little scared now.
The dolphins push Tim with their muzzles in turn.
It doesn't hurt. It just tickles terribly.
Tim has to laugh and laugh because they gently nudge him. It takes some time for the water to get warmer, and Tim can move again.
'Thank you, thank you, dear friends!' Tim calls after them. But they have already disappeared.
All of a sudden, it is quiet. Really quiet.
Tim looks around, and then he realises why the dolphins disappeared so quickly.
There is a huge shark!
It is circling above him. You can recognise sharks immediately by their pointy fins. And by their teeth. And their eyes... Tim thinks they look very nasty.
Everyone knows: you have to get away from here quickly. Tim knows that, too.
The shark has not yet discovered him. And Tim is still too small to not be swallowed by him in one bite.

Tim carefully breathes out air to become heavier. The small bubbles rise, and he slowly sinks deeper. There is a coral reef underneath him. That's where he wants to go as quietly and quickly as possible. The shark above him seems to be elsewhere with his thoughts. Maybe he is asleep because sharks sleep while swimming. Funny too, isn't it?
Tim can't do that. He is moving his fins carefully. Tim sinks even deeper and falls into the soft sand at the bottom, slowly turns around, and hardly dares to look up.
Oh, no – there's a second shark swimming towards the first. Tim paddles very slowly, really slowly, behind a large coral. And there he waits. Ten minutes. Twenty minutes. Half an hour.
The two sharks always circle below the surface of the water. Tim is running out of air.
But he can't show up now.
First, the sharks have to swim away. He hears a hum. A large shadow comes racing up to the surface of the water. It's superfast and super loud! The sharks take flight. This big thing makes a scary noise, and it's very fast. It is so fast that it will soon no longer be heard. What is that? Tim doesn't know.

Tim doesn't want to swim to the surface of the ocean. The two sharks or that loud black thing can come back anytime. And that's why Tim would love to leave this place. He dives through the corals and creeps across the seaweed meadows. It's no use.
He has to swim to the surface to breathe fresh air. Tim closes his eyes and just swims off.
But once he is on the surface, there is nothing to see. No black thing and luckily no shark either. Only the beautiful blue water, waves, and the slightly lighter blue sky above him with a few little clouds dancing on. Tim takes a few breaths and fills his lungs again before the next dive. Tim feels near to starving to death from all the excitement he survived.
Off to the next seaweed meadow.
He dives deeper down. He arrives at the seabed. Tim eats a large amount of seaweed.
It is fresh and juicy.
'Manta, manta!'
Tim lifts his head. Where did that come from?
'Manta, manta!' it calls directly behind him.
Tim turns around.
'Manta, manta! Get out of the way, kid!
Hoho, here, I'm coming!'

Tim watches the huge shadow of a colossal monster fish. That is a fish, isn't it?
One flap of the fins – and this fish has huge fins – and Tim swirls through the current around its own axis.

'Can't you pay attention and be a little more careful, please?' Tim calls after him.

'Manta, manta?'
The gentle giant turns around and comes towards him. Then he hovers above Tim. Tim is already getting a little scared again.
'Who's talking to me? Manta, manta!' the giant asks.
'Down here. It is me! My name is Tim, Tim Turtel. You can't just jet through the water like that. That's dangerous.'
'Hello, I'm Manni. Why do you think I called you, manta, manta? To get you out of the way, kid.'
'Yes, but, but...' Tim has to think for a moment.
'You're swimming much too fast. That is not enough to move out of your way, Manni. Apart from that, I've never seen anyone like you here before.'
The gentle giant, Manni, sinks in the water, a bit like an elevator.

'Manta, manta! Tim, I'm a manta. And we do it like this. What are you doing here anyway? Because I've never seen you here either.'
Tim is a bit embarrassed now because Manni is right.
'Yes, sorry. I'm new here.'
'Manta, manta! Good. Now you know when I'm calling, you have to swim a bit to the side. I have to move a lot because I need a lot of plankton. And the best way for me to get enough of it is to swim very fast.'

'Oh, I didn't know that,' says Tim, looking at Manni.

'I will pay attention to that in the future. I still have one question, dear Manni.'
Tim is still looking at the gentle giant.
'Manta, manta! Which one?'
'How do you manage to be so big? And from so mini, mini little plankton things to eat? I can hardly see them.'
Manni laughs loudly.
'Manta, manta! That works very well. Look up quickly, little Tim. This one also feeds on plankton.
And he's much bigger than me. Manta, manta! Mr. Colleague!' Manni greets him.
And Tim marvels at the big blue whale.

'Wooooosh wooooh chrrrr uuuiiiiaaaa!' the blue whale sings.
Tim covers his ears. He doesn't understand what Mr. Whale is singing up there.
But that doesn't matter.
He marvels again at the huge whale and waves after the manta ray, who is soon no longer visible in the depths of the sea.
He only hears softly
'Manta, manta! Goodbye, little Tim!'

The years are dropping by. Tim has grown up to be
a big and strong sea turtle man.
Meanwhile, Tim is now twenty-five years old
and twenty inches long.

Tim knows every corner of the world's oceans.
Except for the areas of the oceans that
are too cold for him, of course.
Only once, he met another sea turtle of his kind.
Tom was his name, and like Tim, he was born
on a Caribbean beach. Tom didn't like to talk much
and moved forward after a few days.
For a couple of nights, Tim has been dreaming
of having a family of his own.

And something draws him back to the waters of his
homeland, where he hatched a long, long time ago.
And that is why Tim is now setting out.
He looks for a suitable current and lets himself back
to his homeland beach in the Caribbean Sea.
Every night, he dreams about meeting an adorable
young sea turtle.

A female, of course, because he is a male.

'Hi, sea turtle man.' It sounds above him.
Tim looks up. 'Hi. Who are you? Nice to meet you. My name is Tim, Tim Turtel.'
His voice has become much deeper now as he is an adult. It's almost like the voice of Manni, the manta he met.
'You're a free spirit. It shows.' The skate girl giggles.
'I'm Rita.' 'And what's it to, Rita?' he growls back.
'Oh, come on, Tim. We both know where you want to go. And I sincerely wish you every success. Do you even know how to get a sea turtle lady?'
Tim is thinking for a moment.
This fish likes to bully him with words.
Then he calmly answers, 'My instinct will know, Rita. It has helped me in every life situation up to now. I remember.'
'Well, if you think that's enough...' Rita smiles at Tim with a twinkle in her eye.
'Yes. I mean, that's enough, Rita. Maybe that's even complicated only with your kind of fish.' Tim grins broadly at Rita.
'Phhht, such impudence!' hisses Rita, and she burrows herself deep into the sand, just like
how other skate ladies do if they are not amused.

Tim is now almost reaching his final destination.
And he thinks a lot about what Rita said to him.
How does a male sea turtle learn to know
a sea turtle woman?
And how does he know that she likes him too?
And – very important too – how does he
know he likes her?
Does he have to bring her a bunch of fresh seaweed?
Or sing her a song?
Tim has absolutely no idea about this.

What should he do?
That's why he hides for a while until he comes up
with something. He is hoping.
Tim is trying to sleep, but he does not want
to succeed. He is not hungry either.
Something drives him on to swim to his homeland beach.
At the same time, he doesn't want to go any further.
He would rather bury himself in insecurity.

But he is not a skate fish, and he is not a whale
who can effortlessly dive deep under the thick
North Pole ice floes where no one would find him…
to hide there forever.

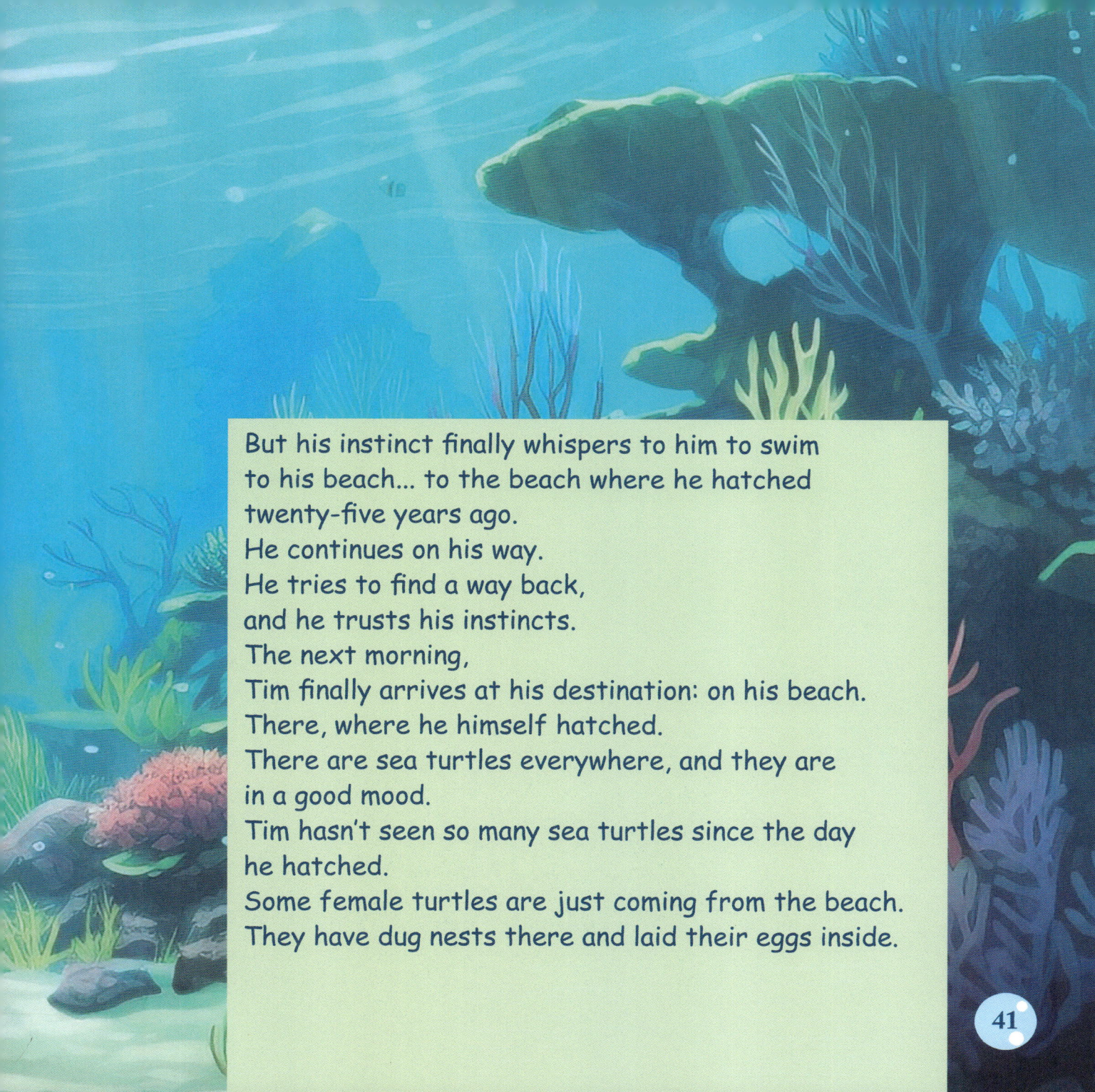

But his instinct finally whispers to him to swim
to his beach... to the beach where he hatched
twenty-five years ago.
He continues on his way.
He tries to find a way back,
and he trusts his instincts.
The next morning,
Tim finally arrives at his destination: on his beach.
There, where he himself hatched.
There are sea turtles everywhere, and they are
in a good mood.
Tim hasn't seen so many sea turtles since the day
he hatched.
Some female turtles are just coming from the beach.
They have dug nests there and laid their eggs inside.

Out in the sea, the males are waiting for them to accompany them to the next beach.

And then Tim sees her: Tamina Tortuga.

She is a beauty from the Mexican Gulf.
Tamina smiles at Tim.

His instinct tells him exactly what to do first.
And the two sea turtles swim into the sea together without saying a single word.
They both know what to do now and what will happen next. And this is their secret.
From now on, Tim comes back to his beach every year. And he is on the lookout for Tamina every time.
Tim goes once again to his nest
and whispers to the eggs,
'Trust your instincts and listen to your gut!
And you will grow up like me.'
Two months later, all the baby sea turtles hatch from the nest. There are almost a hundred small baby turtle eggs in the nest.
Maybe one of them will be called Tim or Tamina.

Thank You!

Without my daughter,
this little book would never have existed.

And without my husband,
I wouldn't have found my courage.

Squirrel Fluff

Fluff is the fluffiest squirrel boy the world has ever seen, and he's still small and terribly cute. That doesn't stop him from having a great adventure in the forest.

This only happens because he won't listen to his parents and runs off into the forest on his own.

In the forest, he finds new friends, the fox Snub and the rabbit Snowball. But Fluff also has to hold his own against cheeky and nasty racoons and spend a night alone in the forest.

Soon available:

Doris Kluin

Squirrel Fluff
And his adventures in the forest

ISBN 978-3-911121-03-3

Recommendation
A read-aloud book for children aged 3 years and older
As a self-reading book for children aged 7 years and older

Printed in Poland
by Amazon Fulfillment
Poland Sp. z o.o., Wrocław

29535925R00025